THIS BOOK BELONGS TO

_____

START DATE

_____

SHE READS TRUTH

EXECUTIVE

FOUNDER/CHIEF EXECUTIVE OFFICER
Raechel Myers

CO-FOUNDER/CHIEF CONTENT OFFICER
Amanda Bible Williams

CHIEF OPERATING OFFICER
Ryan Myers

EDITORIAL

CONTENT DIRECTOR
Jessica Lamb

DIGITAL MANAGING EDITOR
Oghosa Iyamu, MDiv

PRODUCTION EDITOR
Hannah Little, MTS

MARKETING CONTENT EDITOR
Tameshia Williams, ThM

ASSOCIATE EDITOR
Lindsey Jacobi, MDiv

MARKETING

MARKETING DIRECTOR
Kamron Kunce

GROWTH MARKETING MANAGER
Blake Showalter

PRODUCT MARKETING MANAGER
Megan Phillips

SOCIAL MEDIA STRATEGIST
Taylor Krupp

CREATIVE

CREATIVE DIRECTOR
Amy Dennis

DESIGN MANAGER
Kelsea Allen

DESIGNERS
Abbey Benson
Amanda Brush, MA
Annie Glover
Lauren Haag

JUNIOR DESIGNER
Jessie Gerakinis

OPERATIONS

OPERATIONS DIRECTOR
Allison Sutton

OFFICE MANAGER
Nicole Quirion

PROJECT ASSISTANT
Mary Beth Montgomery

SHIPPING

SHIPPING MANAGER
Marian Byne

FULFILLMENT LEAD
Cait Baggerman

FULFILLMENT SPECIALIST
Kajsa Matheny

SUBSCRIPTION INQUIRIES
orders@shereadstruth.com

COMMUNITY SUPPORT

COMMUNITY EXPERIENCE DIRECTOR
Kara Hewett, MOL

COMMUNITY SUPPORT SPECIALISTS
Katy McKnight
Heather Vollono
Margot Williams

CONTRIBUTOR

SPECIAL THANKS
Beth Joseph

SHE READS TRUTH™

© 2023 by She Reads Truth, LLC

All rights reserved.

All photography used by permission.

ISBN 978-1-952670-77-0

1 2 3 4 5 6 7 8 9 10

All Scripture is taken from the Christian Standard Bible®. Copyright © 2020 by Holman Bible Publishers. Used by permission. Christian Standard Bible® and CSB® are federally registered trademarks of Holman Bible Publishers.

Though the locations in this book have been carefully researched, scholars disagree on the precise location of certain places.

Research support provided by Logos Bible Software™. Learn more at logos.com.

@SHEREADSTRUTH

Download the She Reads Truth app, available for iOS and Android

   Subscribe to the She Reads Truth podcast

This book was printed offset in Nashville, Tennessee, on 70# Lynx Opaque. Cover is 100# Cougar Opaque with a soft touch lamination.

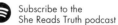

AMOS

The book of Amos gives us God's view of justice and righteousness.

Tameshia Williams, ThM
MARKETING CONTENT
EDITOR

The first time I visited the National Museum of African-American History and Culture, I wept. All that the museum offers beautifully and evocatively captures both the lament and celebration of current and historical moments. From the galleries filled with artifacts and interactive exhibits to the comfort of the restaurant's multi-regional soul food cooking to the spaces thoughtfully designed for reflection and contemplation.

One of these spaces—called the Contemplative Court—is a large room with a wide, round opening at the top. A waterfall pours from this opening all the way down into a pool bordered by long, high-back marble benches. Each wall in the Contemplative Court, coppery bronze and overlaid with glass, bears a quote from a key historical figure. On one wall is a famous quote from Martin Luther King, Jr., which echoes a well-known verse from the book of Amos: "We are determined to work and fight until justice runs down like water and righteousness like a mighty stream." Whenever I visit, I make sure to sit on the bench facing that wall so the quote appears behind the waterfall. The sight and sound of streaming water create a powerful experience, intensifying my longing for the reality of those words. That image kept coming to mind as our team created this reading plan.

The book of Amos gives us God's view of justice and righteousness, primarily through Israel's failure to practice them. They have exploited the poor for economic benefit. They have ignored and mistreated the most vulnerable members of their communities. And they have committed idolatry and other sinful actions. The imagery and sharp tone of Amos carry strong emotion, revealing God's heart of righteousness and justice for all people. While God's judgment warns punishment, it is also a prompt to return to Him. He shouts in Amos 5:4, "Seek me and live!"

That's the call that rings throughout the centuries to us today. The book of Amos invites us to sit in the tension of the brokenness we have experienced and even perpetuated. But it's not for guilt's sake. God's imperative to "let justice flow like water, and righteousness, like an unfailing stream" (Amos 5:24) is an invitation to life!

In this Study Book, we've provided guiding prompts and space for you to reflect on your reading. I pray that during your time in the book of Amos you'll also be prompted to lament the ways that you have turned from God and lean into Him even more. And that you would ultimately experience the refreshing, freeing, joyful, and abundant life that only God can give.

Design
on Purpose

At She Reads Truth, we believe in pairing the inherently beautiful Word of God with the aesthetic beauty it deserves. Each of our resources is thoughtfully and artfully designed to highlight the beauty, goodness, and truth of Scripture in a way that reflects the themes of each curated reading plan.

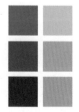

ABCDEFGHI
JKLMNOPQR
STUVWXYZ
1234567890

abcdefghi
jklmnopqr
stuvwxyz
1234567890

The message of Amos is powerful and bold, and the design for this book was chosen to match. The attention-grabbing sans serif font is meant to evoke God's "roar" in Amos 1:2 and the challenging prophecies Amos delivers. Both the rich and muted tones of the color palette remind us of the fullness of life with God in contrast to the sin and shame we experience apart from Him.

In the design concept of this Study Book, nothing is as it should be. The broken shapes and lines on each day reflect the rebellion of God's people and the consequences of their sin, representing how we (and the people of Amos) are in need of repair. Once orderly shapes and design elements are altered with breaks, distortion, and messiness to show the deteriorating consequences of sin. The shapes are off-kilter, but not unfixable.

As each week in the reading plan progresses, the shapes become less fractured and begin to be repaired to reflect the promised restoration of returning to God. The disoriented, disconnected shapes become whole by the end of each week as a reminder that God is able to restore what has been damaged by sin. Perfectly intact lines and symmetrical circles and rectangles represent the wholeness and peace of life in God.

HOW TO USE THIS BOOK

She Reads Truth is a community of women dedicated to reading the Word of God every day. In this **Amos** reading plan, we will read Amos, along with complementary passages of Scripture, as we explore God's heart of righteousness and justice for all people.

READ & REFLECT

Your **Amos** Study Book focuses primarily on Scripture, with added features to come alongside your time with God's Word.

SCRIPTURE READING

Designed for a Monday start, this Study Book presents the book of Amos in daily readings, along with additional passages curated to show how themes from the main reading can be found throughout Scripture.

🍂 *Additional passages are marked in your daily reading with the Going Deeper heading.*

RESPONSE AND REFLECTION

This reading plan begins with prompts to guide your reading and concludes with questions and space for reflection.

COMMUNITY & CONVERSATION

You can start reading this book at any time! If you want to join women from Tallahassee to Turkey as they read along with you, the She Reads Truth community will start Day 1 of **Amos** on Monday, May 22, 2023.

 ## SHE READS TRUTH APP

Devotionals corresponding to each daily reading can be found in the **Amos** reading plan on the She Reads Truth app. New devotionals will be published each weekday once the plan begins on Monday, May 22, 2023. You can use the app to participate in community discussion and more.

GRACE DAY

Use Saturdays to catch up on your reading, pray, and rest in the presence of the Lord.

WEEKLY TRUTH

Sundays are set aside for Scripture memorization.

See tips for memorizing Scripture on page 76.

EXTRAS

This book features additional tools to help you gain a deeper understanding of the text.

Find a complete list of extras on page 11.

 SHEREADSTRUTH.COM

The **Amos** reading plan and devotionals will also be available at SheReadsTruth.com as the community reads each day. Invite your family, friends, and neighbors to read along with you!

 SHE READS TRUTH PODCAST

Subscribe to the She Reads Truth podcast and join our founders and their guests each week as they talk about what you'll read in the week ahead.

 Podcast episodes 178–179 for our **Amos** *series release on Mondays beginning May 22, 2023.*

Table of
Contents

Key Verse _____

"But let justice
flow like water, and
righteousness, like
an unfailing stream."

AMOS 5:24

She Reads Amos

TIME TO
READ AMOS
24 Minutes

ON THE TIMELINE

Amos prophesied after a civil war divided the nation into the northern kingdom, Israel, and the southern kingdom, Judah. His ministry took place during the reigns of King Uzziah of Judah (792–740 BC) and King Jeroboam II of Israel (793–753 BC). This was a time of great prosperity for both nations, and the weakened condition of their enemies meant great military success. Amos's prophecy to Israel occurred around 760 BC, about forty years before Israel was destroyed by Assyria and approximately 175 years before Judah's destruction and exile by Babylon.

A LITTLE BACKGROUND

Amos was a shepherd from Tekoa, a village about ten miles south of Jerusalem in Judah. God called Amos to go north and prophesy against Samaria and the kingdom of Israel. Though we do not know how long he was in the north, it appears to have been a fairly short time. Amos provoked a great deal of opposition and anger, as illustrated by his encounter with Amaziah, the priest of Bethel (Am 7:10–17). He wrote his book, a summary of his prophecies, after his return to Judah.

MESSAGE AND PURPOSE

God's right to judge the earth was the centerpiece of Amos's message. He proclaimed that God is impartial and fair, judging each nation appropriately, and neither Israel, Judah, or any other nation is exempt from divine judgment. In Amos's prophecies, the Gentiles are punished for their crimes against humanity, while the Jewish people are judged by the demands of the Mosaic law (Am 1:3–2:5). Even after judgment, when it seems all hope is lost (Am 9:1–4), God promises to bring about redemption and salvation (Am 9:13–15). Amos prophesies that Israel's hope—and humanity's hope—is in the line of David, which God will raise up to establish His kingdom (Am 9:11–12). We now know this prophecy is fulfilled in Jesus Christ.

GIVE THANKS FOR THE BOOK OF AMOS

The book of Amos reminds us of the sovereignty of God in His involvement with His people. Amos emphasizes the coming Day of the Lord—a day which not only calls all people to account, but also boasts the hope and glory of Christ's return.

Prophets and Prophecy

In order to discern the meaning of these messages, we should first understand them in their original setting.

The prophets delivered God's messages to Israel, Judah, and other ancient Near Eastern societies using relevant historical, geographical, political, and cultural context.

Old Testament prophecy is relational.

Although the prophetic books often deal with concepts like famine, displacement, and God's judgment, the existence of these books shows that God deals with His people and other nations in the context of relationship.

Books of prophecy are collections of allegories, parables, prose, sermons, oracles, prayers, poetry, and short narrative episodes.

While they are organized into sections and categories, books of prophecy should not be taken as collectively chronological or plot driven, as narrative literature is. These works frequently include literary devices to communicate literal truth. For example, the book of Amos uses rhetorical questions (Am 3:3–8; 6:12), metaphor (Am 3:8), irony (Am 4:4–5), simile (Am 5:6), and other literary techniques for emphasis.

God's attributes are wholly present throughout every one of His messages.

God is not sometimes loving and sometimes just, nor is there a hierarchy of His traits. He is all of His attributes all of the time. Though His unique attributes can be identified separately, His essence remains undivided. When reading passages that emphasize one attribute, remember that all other aspects of who God is also remain true.

The darker prophecy gets, the brighter the cross appears.

The bleak imagery of the Old Testament prophets shows the seriousness of sin and the reality that people are without hope outside of a redeemer. Christ went to the cross to atone for the darkest realities described in the prophetic books.

Justice & Righteousness

In the book of Amos, God makes His voice heard,
calling all people to repent from their evil and
seek life in Him. God is just and righteous,
and He calls His people to reflect and
pursue justice and righteousness
in our lives.

As you read each day, take note of
how these concepts are developed
in Amos's prophetic message.

Highlight examples of
justice and injustice.
Underline examples
of righteousness
and unrighteousness.

At the end of your time in the book of
Amos on page 68, space will be provided
for you to reflect on what you have read
and observed about these two
main themes.

JUSTICE

Right judgment
and right action
toward humanity

RIGHTEOUSNESS

An adherence
to God's moral,
upright standard

The LORD roars from Zion
and makes his voice heard
from Jerusalem…
AMOS 1:2

His Voice Is Heard

Use the prompts on p. 17 to make notes as you read.

AMOS 1

¹ The words of Amos, who was one of the sheep breeders from Tekoa—what he saw regarding Israel in the days of King Uzziah of Judah and Jeroboam son of Jehoash, king of Israel, two years before the earthquake.

² He said:

The LORD roars from Zion
and makes his voice heard from Jerusalem;
the pastures of the shepherds mourn,
and the summit of Carmel withers.

JUDGMENT ON ISRAEL'S NEIGHBORS

³ The LORD says:

I will not relent from punishing Damascus
for three crimes, even four,
because they threshed Gilead with iron sledges.
⁴ Therefore, I will send fire against Hazael's palace,
and it will consume Ben-hadad's citadels.
⁵ I will break down the gates of Damascus.
I will cut off the ruler from the Valley of Aven,
and the one who wields the scepter from Beth-eden.
The people of Aram will be exiled to Kir.
The LORD has spoken.

⁶ The LORD says:

I will not relent from punishing Gaza
for three crimes, even four,
because they exiled a whole community,
handing them over to Edom.
⁷ Therefore, I will send fire against the walls of Gaza,
and it will consume its citadels.
⁸ I will cut off the ruler from Ashdod,
and the one who wields the scepter from Ashkelon.
I will also turn my hand against Ekron,
and the remainder of the Philistines will perish.
The Lord GOD has spoken.

⁹ The LORD says:

I will not relent from punishing Tyre
for three crimes, even four,
because they handed over
a whole community of exiles to Edom
and broke a treaty of brotherhood.
¹⁰ Therefore, I will send fire against the walls of Tyre,
and it will consume its citadels.

[11] The Lord says:

I will not relent from punishing Edom
for three crimes, even four,
because he pursued his brother with the sword.
He stifled his compassion,
his anger tore at him continually,
and he harbored his rage incessantly.
[12] Therefore, I will send fire against Teman,
and it will consume the citadels of Bozrah.

[13] The Lord says:

I will not relent from punishing the Ammonites
for three crimes, even four,
because they ripped open
the pregnant women of Gilead
in order to enlarge their territory.
[14] Therefore, I will set fire to the walls of Rabbah,
and it will consume its citadels.
There will be shouting on the day of battle
and a violent wind on the day of the storm.
[15] Their king and his princes
will go into exile together.
The Lord has spoken.

AMOS 2:1–3

[1] The Lord says:

I will not relent from punishing Moab
for three crimes, even four,
because he burned the bones
of the king of Edom to lime.
[2] Therefore, I will send fire against Moab,
and it will consume the citadels of Kerioth.
Moab will die with a tumult,
with shouting and the sound of the ram's horn.
[3] I will cut off the judge from the land
and kill all its officials with him.
The Lord has spoken.

🛡 GOING DEEPER

PSALM 33:13–22

[13] The Lord looks down from heaven;
he observes everyone.
[14] He gazes on all the inhabitants of the earth
from his dwelling place.
[15] He forms the hearts of them all;
he considers all their works.
[16] A king is not saved by a large army;
a warrior will not be rescued by great strength.
[17] The horse is a false hope for safety;
it provides no escape by its great power.

[18] But look, the Lord keeps his eye on those who fear him—
those who depend on his faithful love
[19] to rescue them from death
and to keep them alive in famine.

[20] We wait for the Lord;
he is our help and shield.
[21] For our hearts rejoice in him
because we trust in his holy name.
[22] May your faithful love rest on us, Lord,
for we put our hope in you.

ROMANS 1:16–23

THE RIGHTEOUS WILL LIVE BY FAITH

[16] For I am not ashamed of the gospel, because it is the power of God for salvation to everyone who believes, first to the Jew, and also to the Greek. [17] For in it the righteousness of God is revealed from faith to faith, just as it is written: The righteous will live by faith.

THE GUILT OF THE GENTILE WORLD

[18] For God's wrath is revealed from heaven against all godlessness and unrighteousness of people who by their unrighteousness suppress the truth, [19] since what can be known about God is evident among them, because God has

shown it to them. [20] For his invisible attributes, that is, his eternal power and divine nature, have been clearly seen since the creation of the world, being understood through what he has made. As a result, people are without excuse. [21] For though they knew God, they did not glorify him as God or show gratitude. Instead, their thinking became worthless, and their senseless hearts were darkened. [22] Claiming to be wise, they became fools [23] and exchanged the glory of the immortal God for images resembling mortal man, birds, four-footed animals, and reptiles.

NOTES

Led Astray by Lies

AMOS 2:4–16

JUDGMENT ON JUDAH

⁴ The LORD says:

I will not relent from punishing Judah
for three crimes, even four,
because they have rejected the instruction of the LORD
and have not kept his statutes.
The lies that their ancestors followed
have led them astray.
⁵ Therefore, I will send fire against Judah,
and it will consume the citadels of Jerusalem.

JUDGMENT ON ISRAEL

⁶ The LORD says:

I will not relent from punishing Israel
for three crimes, even four,
because they sell a righteous person for silver
and a needy person for a pair of sandals.
⁷ They trample the heads of the poor
on the dust of the ground
and obstruct the path of the needy.
A man and his father have sexual relations
with the same girl,
profaning my holy name.
⁸ They stretch out beside every altar
on garments taken as collateral,
and in the house of their God
they drink wine obtained through fines.

⁹ Yet I destroyed the Amorite as Israel advanced;
his height was like the cedars,
and he was as sturdy as the oaks;

I destroyed his fruit above and his roots beneath.
¹⁰ And I brought you from the land of Egypt
and led you forty years in the wilderness
in order to possess the land of the Amorite.
¹¹ I raised up some of your sons as prophets
and some of your young men as Nazirites.
Is this not the case, Israelites?

> This is the LORD's declaration.

¹² But you made the Nazirites drink wine
and commanded the prophets,
"Do not prophesy."
¹³ Look, I am about to crush you in your place
as a wagon crushes when full of grain.
¹⁴ Escape will fail the swift,
the strong one will not maintain his strength,
and the warrior will not save his life.
¹⁵ The archer will not stand his ground,
the one who is swift of foot
will not save himself,
and the one riding a horse will not save his life.
¹⁶ Even the most courageous of the warriors
will flee naked on that day—

> this is the LORD's declaration.

◖ GOING DEEPER

DEUTERONOMY 6:4–19

⁴ Listen, Israel: The LORD our God, the LORD is one. ⁵ Love the LORD your God with all your heart, with all your soul, and with all your strength.

⁶ These words that I am giving you today are to be in your heart.

⁷ Repeat them to your children. Talk about them when you sit in your house and when you walk along the road, when you lie down and when you get up. ⁸ Bind them as a sign on your hand and let them be a symbol on your forehead. ⁹ Write them on the doorposts of your house and on your city gates.

[10] When the Lord your God brings you into the land he swore to your ancestors Abraham, Isaac, and Jacob that he would give you—a land with large and beautiful cities that you did not build, [11] houses full of every good thing that you did not fill them with, cisterns that you did not dig, and vineyards and olive groves that you did not plant—and when you eat and are satisfied, [12] be careful not to forget the Lord who brought you out of the land of Egypt, out of the place of slavery. [13] Fear the Lord your God, worship him, and take your oaths in his name. [14] Do not follow other gods, the gods of the peoples around you, [15] for the Lord your God, who is among you, is a jealous God. Otherwise, the Lord your God will become angry with you and obliterate you from the face of the earth. [16] Do not test the Lord your God as you tested him at Massah. [17] Carefully observe the commands of the Lord your God, the decrees and statutes he has commanded you. [18] Do what is right and good in the Lord's sight, so that you may prosper and so that you may enter and possess the good land the Lord your God swore to give your ancestors, [19] by driving out all your enemies before you, as the Lord has said.

JAMES 2:1–13

THE SIN OF FAVORITISM

[1] My brothers and sisters, do not show favoritism as you hold on to the faith in our glorious Lord Jesus Christ. [2] For if someone comes into your meeting wearing a gold ring and dressed in fine clothes, and a poor person dressed in filthy clothes also comes in, [3] if you look with favor on the one wearing the fine clothes and say, "Sit here in a good place," and yet you say to the poor person, "Stand over there," or "Sit here on the floor by my footstool," [4] haven't you made distinctions among yourselves and become judges with evil thoughts?

[5] Listen, my dear brothers and sisters: Didn't God choose the poor in this world to be rich in faith and heirs of the kingdom that he has promised to those who love him? [6] Yet you have dishonored the poor. Don't the rich oppress you and drag you into court? [7] Don't they blaspheme the good name that was invoked over you?

[8] Indeed, if you fulfill the royal law prescribed in the Scripture, Love your neighbor as yourself, you are doing well. [9] If, however, you show favoritism, you commit sin and are convicted by the law as transgressors. [10] For whoever keeps the entire law, and yet stumbles at one point, is guilty of breaking it all. [11] For he who said, Do not commit adultery, also said, Do not murder. So if you do not commit adultery, but you murder, you are a lawbreaker.

[12] Speak and act as those who are to be judged by the law of freedom. [13] For judgment is without mercy to the one who has not shown mercy. Mercy triumphs over judgment.

Punishment for Unrighteousness

AMOS 3

GOD'S REASONS FOR PUNISHING ISRAEL

¹ Listen to this message that the LORD has spoken against you, Israelites, against the entire clan that I brought from the land of Egypt:

² I have known only you
out of all the clans of the earth;
therefore, I will punish you for all your iniquities.
³ Can two walk together
without agreeing to meet?
⁴ Does a lion roar in the forest
when it has no prey?
Does a young lion growl from its lair
unless it has captured something?
⁵ Does a bird land in a trap on the ground
if there is no bait for it?
Does a trap spring from the ground
when it has caught nothing?
⁶ If a ram's horn is blown in a city,
aren't people afraid?
If a disaster occurs in a city,
hasn't the LORD done it?
⁷ Indeed, the Lord GOD does nothing
without revealing his counsel
to his servants the prophets.
⁸ A lion has roared;
who will not fear?
The Lord GOD has spoken;
who will not prophesy?

⁹ Proclaim on the citadels in Ashdod
and on the citadels in the land of Egypt:
Assemble on the mountains of Samaria,
and see the great turmoil in the city
and the acts of oppression within it.
¹⁰ The people are incapable of doing right—
this is the Lord's declaration—
those who store up violence and destruction
in their citadels.

¹¹ Therefore, the Lord God says:

An enemy will surround the land;
he will destroy your strongholds
and plunder your citadels.

¹² The Lord says:

As the shepherd snatches two legs
or a piece of an ear
from the lion's mouth,
so the Israelites who live in Samaria
will be rescued
with only the corner of a bed
or the cushion of a couch.

¹³ Listen and testify against the house of Jacob—
this is the declaration of the Lord God,
the God of Armies.
¹⁴ I will punish the altars of Bethel
on the day I punish Israel for its crimes;
the horns of the altar will be cut off
and fall to the ground.
¹⁵ I will demolish the winter house
and the summer house;
the houses inlaid with ivory will be destroyed,
and the great houses will come to an end.

This is the Lord's declaration.

🔖 GOING DEEPER

ISAIAH 59:12–21

¹² For our transgressions have multiplied before you,
and our sins testify against us.
For our transgressions are with us,
and we know our iniquities:
¹³ transgression and deception against the Lord,
turning away from following our God,
speaking oppression and revolt,
conceiving and uttering lying words from the heart.
¹⁴ Justice is turned back,
and righteousness stands far off.
For truth has stumbled in the public square,
and honesty cannot enter.
¹⁵ Truth is missing,
and whoever turns from evil is plundered.
The Lord saw that there was no justice,
and he was offended.
¹⁶ He saw that there was no man—
he was amazed that there was no one interceding;
so his own arm brought salvation,
and his own righteousness supported him.

¹⁷ He put on righteousness as body armor,
and a helmet of salvation on his head;
he put on garments of vengeance for clothing,
and he wrapped himself in zeal as in a cloak.
¹⁸ So he will repay according to their deeds:
fury to his enemies,
retribution to his foes,
and he will repay the coasts and islands.
¹⁹ They will fear the name of the Lord in the west
and his glory in the east;
for he will come like a rushing stream
driven by the wind of the Lord.
²⁰ "The Redeemer will come to Zion,
and to those in Jacob who turn from transgression."
This is the Lord's declaration.

[21] "As for me, this is my covenant with them," says the LORD: "My Spirit who is on you, and my words that I have put in your mouth, will not depart from your mouth, or from the mouths of your children, or from the mouths of your children's children, from now on and forever," says the LORD.

TITUS 3:1–11

CHRISTIAN LIVING AMONG OUTSIDERS

[1] Remind them to submit to rulers and authorities, to obey, to be ready for every good work, [2] to slander no one, to avoid fighting, and to be kind, always showing gentleness to all people. [3] For we too were once foolish, disobedient, deceived, enslaved by various passions and pleasures, living in malice and envy, hateful, detesting one another.

[4] But when the kindness of God our Savior and his love for mankind appeared,

[5] he saved us—not by works of righteousness that we had done, but according to his mercy—through the washing of regeneration and renewal by the Holy Spirit.

[6] He poured out his Spirit on us abundantly through Jesus Christ our Savior [7] so that, having been justified by his grace, we may become heirs with the hope of eternal life. [8] This saying is trustworthy. I want you to insist on these things, so that those who have believed God might be careful to devote themselves to good works. These are good and profitable for everyone. [9] But avoid foolish debates, genealogies, quarrels, and disputes about the law, because they are unprofitable and worthless. [10] Reject a divisive person after a first and second warning. [11] For you know that such a person has gone astray and is sinning; he is self-condemned.

NOTES

A Call to Repentance

"Yet you did not return to me."
AMOS 4:6

SOCIAL AND SPIRITUAL CORRUPTION

¹ Listen to this message, you cows of Bashan
who are on the hill of Samaria,
women who oppress the poor
and crush the needy,
who say to their husbands,
"Bring us something to drink."

² The Lord God has sworn by his holiness:

Look, the days are coming
when you will be taken away with hooks,
every last one of you with fishhooks.
³ You will go through breaches in the wall,
each woman straight ahead,
and you will be driven along toward Harmon.
    This is the Lord's declaration.

⁴ Come to Bethel and rebel;
rebel even more at Gilgal!
Bring your sacrifices every morning,
your tenths every three days.
⁵ Offer leavened bread as a thanksgiving sacrifice,
and loudly proclaim your freewill offerings,
for that is what you Israelites love to do!

    This is the declaration of the Lord God.

GOD'S DISCIPLINE AND ISRAEL'S APOSTASY

⁶ I gave you absolutely nothing to eat in all your cities,
a shortage of food in all your communities,
yet you did not return to me.
    This is the Lord's declaration.

⁷ I also withheld the rain from you
while there were still three months until harvest.

I sent rain on one city
but no rain on another.
One field received rain
while a field with no rain withered.
⁸ Two or three cities staggered
to another city to drink water
but were not satisfied,
yet you did not return to me.
    This is the Lord's declaration.

⁹ I struck you with blight and mildew;
the locust devoured
your many gardens and vineyards,
your fig trees and olive trees,
yet you did not return to me.
    This is the Lord's declaration.

¹⁰ I sent plagues like those of Egypt;
I killed your young men with the sword,
along with your captured horses.
I caused the stench of your camp
to fill your nostrils,
yet you did not return to me.
    This is the Lord's declaration.

¹¹ I overthrew some of you
as I overthrew Sodom and Gomorrah,
and you were like a burning stick
snatched from a fire,
yet you did not return to me—
    This is the Lord's declaration.

¹² Therefore, Israel, that is what I will do to you,
and since I will do that to you,
Israel, prepare to meet your God!

[13] He is here:
the one who forms the mountains,
creates the wind,
and reveals his thoughts to man,
the one who makes the dawn out of darkness
and strides on the heights of the earth.
The Lord, the God of Armies, is his name.

GOING DEEPER

HOSEA 6:1–3

A CALL TO REPENTANCE

[1] Come, let's return to the Lord.
For he has torn us,
and he will heal us;
he has wounded us,
and he will bind up our wounds.
[2] He will revive us after two days,
and on the third day he will raise us up
so we can live in his presence.
[3] Let's strive to know the Lord.
His appearance is as sure as the dawn.
He will come to us like the rain,
like the spring showers that water the land.

HOSEA 10:12

Sow righteousness for yourselves
and reap faithful love;
break up your unplowed ground.
It is time to seek the Lord
until he comes and sends righteousness
on you like the rain.

HEBREWS 12:1–14

THE CALL TO ENDURANCE

[1] Therefore, since we also have such a large cloud of witnesses surrounding us, let us lay aside every hindrance and the sin that so easily ensnares us. Let us run with endurance the race that lies before us, [2] keeping our eyes on Jesus, the pioneer and perfecter of our faith. For the joy that lay before him, he endured the cross,

despising the shame, and sat down at the right hand of the throne of God.

FATHERLY DISCIPLINE

³ For consider him who endured such hostility from sinners against himself, so that you won't grow weary and give up. ⁴ In struggling against sin, you have not yet resisted to the point of shedding your blood. ⁵ And you have forgotten the exhortation that addresses you as sons:

> My son, do not take the Lord's
>   discipline lightly
> or lose heart when you are reproved
>   by him,
> ⁶ for the Lord disciplines the one he loves
> and punishes every son he receives.

⁷ Endure suffering as discipline: God is dealing with you as sons. For what son is there that a father does not discipline? ⁸ But if you are without discipline—which all receive—then you are illegitimate children and not sons. ⁹ Furthermore, we had human fathers discipline us, and we respected them. Shouldn't we submit even more to the Father of spirits and live? ¹⁰ For they disciplined us for a short time based on what seemed good to them, but he does it for our benefit, so that we can share his holiness. ¹¹ No discipline seems enjoyable at the time, but painful. Later on, however, it yields the peaceful fruit of righteousness to those who have been trained by it.

¹² Therefore, strengthen your tired hands and weakened knees, ¹³ and make straight paths for your feet, so that what is lame may not be dislocated but healed instead.

WARNING AGAINST REJECTING GOD'S GRACE

¹⁴ Pursue peace with everyone, and holiness—without it no one will see the Lord.

NOTES

Seek God and Live

AMOS 5:1–17

LAMENTATION FOR ISRAEL

¹ Listen to this message that I am singing for you, a lament, house of Israel:

² She has fallen;
Virgin Israel will never rise again.
She lies abandoned on her land
with no one to raise her up.

³ For the Lord God says:

The city that marches out a thousand strong
will have only a hundred left,
and the one that marches out a hundred strong
will have only ten left in the house of Israel.

SEEK GOD AND LIVE

⁴ For the Lord says to the house of Israel:

Seek me and live!
⁵ Do not seek Bethel
or go to Gilgal
or journey to Beer-sheba,
for Gilgal will certainly go into exile,
and Bethel will come to nothing.
⁶ Seek the Lord and live,
or he will spread like fire
throughout the house of Joseph;
it will consume everything
with no one at Bethel to extinguish it.
⁷ Those who turn justice into wormwood
also throw righteousness to the ground.

⁸ The one who made the Pleiades and Orion,
who turns darkness into dawn
and darkens day into night,
who summons the water of the sea
and pours it out over the surface of the earth—
the Lord is his name.
⁹ He brings destruction on the strong,
and it falls on the fortress.

¹⁰ They hate the one who convicts the guilty
at the city gate,

NOTES

and they despise the one who speaks with integrity.

¹¹ Therefore, because you trample on the poor
and exact a grain tax from him,
you will never live in the houses of cut stone
you have built;
you will never drink the wine
from the lush vineyards
you have planted.

¹² For I know your crimes are many
and your sins innumerable.
They oppress the righteous, take a bribe,
and deprive the poor of justice at the city gates.

¹³ Therefore, those who have insight will keep silent
at such a time,
for the days are evil.

¹⁴ Pursue good and not evil
so that you may live,
and the Lᴏʀᴅ, the God of Armies,
will be with you
as you have claimed.

¹⁵ Hate evil and love good;
establish justice at the city gate.
Perhaps the Lᴏʀᴅ, the God of Armies, will be gracious
to the remnant of Joseph.

¹⁶ Therefore the Lᴏʀᴅ, the God of Armies, the Lord, says:

There will be wailing in all the public squares;
they will cry out in anguish in all the streets.
The farmer will be called on to mourn,
and professional mourners to wail.

¹⁷ There will be wailing in all the vineyards,
for I will pass among you.
The Lᴏʀᴅ has spoken.

⬛ GOING DEEPER

ISAIAH 55:6–7

**⁶ Seek the Lᴏʀᴅ while he may be found;
call to him while he is near.**

7 Let the wicked one abandon his way
and the sinful one his thoughts;
let him return to the LORD,
so he may have compassion on him,
and to our God, for he will freely forgive.

COLOSSIANS 3:1–17

THE LIFE OF THE NEW MAN

1 So if you have been raised with Christ, seek the things above, where Christ is, seated at the right hand of God. 2 Set your minds on things above, not on earthly things. 3 For you died, and your life is hidden with Christ in God. 4 When Christ, who is your life, appears, then you also will appear with him in glory.

5 Therefore, put to death what belongs to your earthly nature: sexual immorality, impurity, lust, evil desire, and greed, which is idolatry. 6 Because of these, God's wrath is coming upon the disobedient, 7 and you once walked in these things when you were living in them. 8 But now, put away all the following: anger, wrath, malice, slander, and filthy language from your mouth. 9 Do not lie to one another, since you have put off the old self with its practices 10 and have put on the new self. You are being renewed in knowledge according to the image of your Creator. 11 In Christ there is not Greek and Jew, circumcision and uncircumcision, barbarian, Scythian, slave and free; but Christ is all and in all.

THE CHRISTIAN LIFE

12 Therefore, as God's chosen ones, holy and dearly loved, put on compassion, kindness, humility, gentleness, and patience, 13 bearing with one another and forgiving one another if anyone has a grievance against another. Just as the Lord has forgiven you, so you are also to forgive. 14 Above all, put on love, which is the perfect bond of unity. 15 And let the peace of Christ, to which you were also called in one body, rule your hearts. And be thankful. 16 Let the word of Christ dwell richly among you, in all wisdom teaching and admonishing one another through psalms, hymns, and spiritual songs, singing to God with gratitude in your hearts. 17 And whatever you do, in word or in deed, do everything in the name of the Lord Jesus, giving thanks to God the Father through him.

NOTES

We cannot
and must
not soften
the blow; we
cannot and
must not
pretend that
evil isn't that
bad after all.

N. T. Wright
Evil and the Justice of God

Grace Day

Take this day to catch up on
your reading, pray, and rest
in the presence of the Lord.

The LORD looks down from
heaven; he observes everyone.
He gazes on all the inhabitants of
the earth from his dwelling place.
He forms the hearts of them all;
he considers all their works.

Psalm 33:13–15

Weekly Truth

Scripture is God-breathed and true.
When we memorize it, we carry His Word with us wherever we go.

This week we will work to memorize our key verse for the book of Amos, God's declaration for righteousness and justice to flow.

"But let justice flow like water, and righteousness, like an unfailing stream."

Amos 5:24

See tips for memorizing Scripture on page 76.

The Lᴏʀᴅ, the God of Armies,
is his name. He has spoken.
AMOS 5:27

True Worship

Don't forget to use the prompts on p. 17 to make notes as you continue reading.

_____

AMOS 5:18–27

THE DAY OF THE LORD

¹⁸ Woe to you who long for the day of the LORD!
What will the day of the LORD be for you?
It will be darkness and not light.
¹⁹ It will be like a man who flees from a lion
only to have a bear confront him.
He goes home and rests his hand against the wall
only to have a snake bite him.
²⁰ Won't the day of the LORD
be darkness rather than light,
even gloom without any brightness in it?
²¹ I hate, I despise, your feasts!
I can't stand the stench
of your solemn assemblies.
²² Even if you offer me
your burnt offerings and grain offerings,
I will not accept them;
I will have no regard
for your fellowship offerings of fattened cattle.
²³ Take away from me the noise of your songs!
I will not listen to the music of your harps.
²⁴ But let justice flow like water,
and righteousness, like an unfailing stream.

²⁵ "House of Israel, was it sacrifices and grain offerings that you presented to me during the forty years in the wilderness? ²⁶ But you have taken up Sakkuth your king and Kaiwan your star god, images you have made for yourselves. ²⁷ So I will send you into exile beyond Damascus." The LORD, the God of Armies, is his name. He has spoken.

🔖 GOING DEEPER

MICAH 6:1–8

GOD'S LAWSUIT AGAINST JUDAH

¹ Now listen to what the LORD is saying:

Rise, plead your case before the mountains,
and let the hills hear your complaint.
² Listen to the LORD's lawsuit,
you mountains and enduring foundations of the earth,
because the LORD has a case against his people,
and he will argue it against Israel.
³ My people, what have I done to you,
or how have I wearied you?

Testify against me!
⁴ Indeed, I brought you up from the land of Egypt
and redeemed you from that place of slavery.
I sent Moses, Aaron, and Miriam ahead of you.
⁵ My people,
remember what King Balak of Moab proposed,
what Balaam son of Beor answered him,
and what happened from the Acacia Grove to Gilgal
so that you may acknowledge
the Lᴏʀᴅ's righteous acts.

⁶ What should I bring before the Lᴏʀᴅ
when I come to bow before God on high?
Should I come before him with burnt offerings,
with year-old calves?
⁷ Would the Lᴏʀᴅ be pleased with thousands of rams
or with ten thousand streams of oil?
Should I give my firstborn for my transgression,
the offspring of my body for my own sin?

⁸ Mankind, he has told each of you what is good
and what it is the Lᴏʀᴅ requires of you:
to act justly,
to love faithfulness,
and to walk humbly with your God.

MARK 12:28–34

THE PRIMARY COMMANDS

²⁸ One of the scribes approached. When he heard them debating and saw that Jesus answered them well, he asked him, "Which command is the most important of all?"

²⁹ Jesus answered, "The most important is Listen, Israel! The Lord our God, the Lord is one. ³⁰ Love the Lord your God with all your heart, with all your soul, with all your mind, and with all your strength. ³¹ The second is, Love your neighbor as yourself. There is no other command greater than these."

³² Then the scribe said to him, "You are right, teacher. You have correctly said that he is one, and there is no one else except him. ³³ And to love him with all your heart, with all your understanding, and with all your strength, and to love your neighbor as yourself, is far more important than all the burnt offerings and sacrifices."

34 When Jesus saw that he answered wisely, he said to him, "You are not far from the kingdom of God." And no one dared to question him any longer.

2 PETER 3:8–13

8 Dear friends, don't overlook this one fact: With the Lord one day is like a thousand years, and a thousand years like one day. 9 The Lord does not delay his promise, as some understand delay, but is patient with you, not wanting any to perish but all to come to repentance.

10 But the day of the Lord will come like a thief; on that day the heavens will pass away with a loud noise, the elements will burn and be dissolved, and the earth and the works on it will be disclosed. 11 Since all these things are to be dissolved in this way,

it is clear what sort of people you should be in holy conduct and godliness

12 as you wait for the day of God and hasten its coming. Because of that day, the heavens will be dissolved with fire and the elements will melt with heat. 13 But based on his promise, we wait for new heavens and a new earth, where righteousness dwells.

Judgment Against Pride

"I loathe Jacob's pride…"
AMOS 6:8

WOE TO THE COMPLACENT

¹ Woe to those who are at ease in Zion
and to those who feel secure on the hill of Samaria—
the notable people in this first of the nations,
those the house of Israel comes to.
² Cross over to Calneh and see;
go from there to great Hamath;
then go down to Gath of the Philistines.
Are you better than these kingdoms?
Is their territory larger than yours?
³ You dismiss any thought of the evil day
and bring in a reign of violence.

⁴ They lie on beds inlaid with ivory,
sprawled out on their couches,
and dine on lambs from the flock
and calves from the stall.
⁵ They improvise songs to the sound of the harp
and invent their own musical instruments like David.
⁶ They drink wine by the bowlful
and anoint themselves with the finest oils
but do not grieve over the ruin of Joseph.
⁷ Therefore, they will now go into exile
as the first of the captives,
and the feasting of those who sprawl out
will come to an end.

ISRAEL'S PRIDE JUDGED

⁸ The Lord GOD has sworn by himself—this is the declaration
of the LORD, the God of Armies:

I loathe Jacob's pride
and hate his citadels,
so I will hand over the city and everything in it.

⁹ And if there are ten men left in one house, they will die.
¹⁰ A close relative and burner will remove his corpse from the house. He will call to someone in the inner recesses of the house, "Any more with you?"

That person will reply, "None."

Then he will say, "Silence, because the LORD's name must not be invoked."

¹¹ For the LORD commands:

The large house will be smashed to pieces,
and the small house to rubble.

¹² Do horses gallop on the cliffs?
Does anyone plow there with oxen?

Yet you have turned justice into poison
and the fruit of righteousness
    into wormwood—

¹³ you who rejoice over Lo-debar
and say, "Didn't we capture Karnaim
for ourselves by our own strength?"

¹⁴ But look, I am raising up a nation
against you, house of Israel—
    this is the declaration of the Lord,
    the God of Armies—
and they will oppress you
from the entrance of Hamath
to the Brook of the Arabah.

◢ GOING DEEPER

JEREMIAH 22:3–5

³ "This is what the Lord says:

Administer justice and righteousness. Rescue the victim of robbery from his oppressor. Don't exploit or brutalize the resident alien, the fatherless, or the widow. Don't shed innocent blood in this place.

⁴ For if you conscientiously carry out this word, then kings sitting on David's throne will enter through the gates of this palace riding on chariots and horses—they, their officers, and their people. ⁵ But if you do not obey these words, then I swear by myself—this is the Lord's declaration—that this house will become a ruin."

REVELATION 3:14–22

THE LETTER TO LAODICEA

¹⁴ "Write to the angel of the church in Laodicea: Thus says the Amen, the faithful and true witness, the originator of God's creation: ¹⁵ I know your works, that you are neither cold nor hot. I wish that you were cold or hot. ¹⁶ So, because you are lukewarm, and neither hot nor cold, I am going to vomit you out of my mouth. ¹⁷ For you say, 'I'm rich; I have become wealthy and need nothing,' and you don't realize that you are wretched, pitiful, poor, blind, and naked. ¹⁸ I advise you to buy from me gold refined in the fire so that you may be rich, white clothes so that you may be dressed and your shameful nakedness not be exposed, and ointment to spread on your eyes so that you may see. ¹⁹ As many as I love, I rebuke and discipline. So be zealous and repent. ²⁰ See! I stand at the door and knock. If anyone hears my voice and opens the door, I will come in to him and eat with him, and he with me.

²¹ "To the one who conquers I will give the right to sit with me on my throne, just as I also conquered and sat down with my Father on his throne.

²² "Let anyone who has ears to hear listen to what the Spirit says to the churches."

Neighbors of Israel and Judah

DAMASCUS •

ARAM

• TYRE

• DAN

Sea of Galilee

▲ MOUNT CARMEL

Mediterranean Sea

• JABESH-GILEAD

Jordan River

• SAMARIA

ISRAEL

AMMON

• BETHEL

• RABBAH

• EKRON

• JERUSALEM

BETHLEHEM •

• TEKOA

ASHDOD •

• HEBRON

MOAB

ASHKELON •

• KERIOTH

GAZA •

PHILISTIA

Dead Sea

JUDAH

Coastal Highway

• BEERSHEBA

King's Highway

N

EDOM

0 MI   10   20   30   40

BOZRAH •

0 KM   20   40   60

TEMAN •

Opposition to Amos's Prophecy

AMOS 7

FIRST VISION: LOCUSTS

¹ The Lord God showed me this: He was forming a swarm of locusts at the time the spring crop first began to sprout—after the cutting of the king's hay. ² When the locusts finished eating the vegetation of the land, I said, "Lord God, please forgive! How will Jacob survive since he is so small?"

³ The Lord relented concerning this. "It will not happen," he said.

SECOND VISION: FIRE

⁴ The Lord God showed me this: The Lord God was calling for a judgment by fire. It consumed the great deep and devoured the land. ⁵ Then I said, "Lord God, please stop! How will Jacob survive since he is so small?"

⁶ The Lord relented concerning this. "This will not happen either," said the Lord God.

THIRD VISION: A PLUMB LINE

⁷ He showed me this: The Lord was standing there by a vertical wall with a plumb line in his hand. ⁸ The Lord asked me, "What do you see, Amos?"

I replied, "A plumb line."

Then the Lord said, "I am setting a plumb line among my people Israel; I will no longer spare them:

**⁹ Isaac's high places will be deserted,
and Israel's sanctuaries will be in ruins;**

I will rise up against the house of Jeroboam
with a sword."

AMAZIAH'S OPPOSITION

¹⁰ Amaziah the priest of Bethel sent word to King Jeroboam of Israel, saying, "Amos has conspired against you right here in the house of Israel. The land cannot endure all his words, ¹¹ for Amos has said this: 'Jeroboam will die by the sword, and Israel will certainly go into exile from its homeland.'"

¹² Then Amaziah said to Amos, "Go away, you seer! Flee to the land of Judah. Earn your living and give your prophecies there, ¹³ but don't ever prophesy at Bethel again, for it is the king's sanctuary and a royal temple."

¹⁴ So Amos answered Amaziah, "I was not a prophet or the son of a prophet; rather, I was a herdsman, and I took care of sycamore figs. ¹⁵ But the LORD took me from following the flock and said to me, 'Go, prophesy to my people Israel.'"

¹⁶ Now hear the word of the LORD. You say:

> Do not prophesy against Israel;
> do not preach against the house of Isaac.

¹⁷ Therefore, this is what the LORD says:

> Your wife will be a prostitute in the city,
> your sons and daughters will fall by the sword,
> and your land will be divided up
> with a measuring line.
> You yourself will die on pagan soil,
> and Israel will certainly go into exile
> from its homeland.

🔖 GOING DEEPER

ISAIAH 40:6–8

⁶ A voice was saying, "Cry out!"
Another said, "What should I cry out?"
"All humanity is grass,
and all its goodness is like the flower of the field.
⁷ The grass withers, the flowers fade
when the breath of the LORD blows on them;
indeed, the people are grass.

[8] The grass withers, the flowers fade,
but the word of our God remains forever."

2 TIMOTHY 4:1–5

FULFILL YOUR MINISTRY

[1] I solemnly charge you before God and Christ Jesus, who is going to judge the living and the dead, and because of his appearing and his kingdom: [2] Preach the word; be ready in season and out of season; correct, rebuke, and encourage with great patience and teaching. [3] For the time will come when people will not tolerate sound doctrine, but according to their own desires, will multiply teachers for themselves because they have an itch to hear what they want to hear. [4] They will turn away from hearing the truth and will turn aside to myths. [5] But as for you, exercise self-control in everything, endure hardship, do the work of an evangelist, fulfill your ministry.

NOTES

Seeking the Word of the Lord

AMOS 8

FOURTH VISION: A BASKET OF SUMMER FRUIT

[1] The Lord God showed me this: a basket of summer fruit.
[2] He asked me, "What do you see, Amos?"

I replied, "A basket of summer fruit."

The Lord said to me, "The end has come for my people Israel; I will no longer spare them. [3] In that day the temple songs will become wailing"—this is the Lord God's declaration. "Many dead bodies, thrown everywhere! Silence!"

[4] Hear this, you who trample on the needy
and do away with the poor of the land,
[5] asking, "When will the New Moon be over
so we may sell grain,
and the Sabbath,
so we may market wheat?
We can reduce the measure
while increasing the price
and cheat with dishonest scales.
[6] We can buy the poor with silver
and the needy for a pair of sandals
and even sell the chaff!"

[7] The Lord has sworn by the Pride of Jacob:

I will never forget all their deeds.
[8] Because of this, won't the land quake
and all who dwell in it mourn?

All of it will rise like the Nile;
it will surge and then subside
like the Nile in Egypt.

⁹ And in that day—
    this is the declaration of the Lord GOD—
I will make the sun go down at noon;
I will darken the land in the daytime.
¹⁰ I will turn your feasts into mourning
and all your songs into lamentation;
I will cause everyone to wear sackcloth
and every head to be shaved.
I will make that grief
like mourning for an only son
and its outcome like a bitter day.

¹¹ Look, the days are coming—
    this is the declaration of the Lord GOD—
when I will send a famine through the land:
not a famine of bread or a thirst for water,
but of hearing the words of the LORD.
¹² People will stagger from sea to sea
and roam from north to east
seeking the word of the LORD,
but they will not find it.
¹³ In that day the beautiful young women,
the young men also, will faint from thirst.
¹⁴ Those who swear by the guilt of Samaria
and say, "As your god lives, Dan,"
or, "As the way of Beer-sheba lives"—
they will fall, never to rise again.

◤ GOING DEEPER

EXODUS 34:6–7

⁶ The LORD passed in front of him and proclaimed:

The LORD—the LORD is a compassionate and gracious God, slow to anger and abounding in faithful love and truth, ⁷ maintaining faithful love to a thousand generations, forgiving iniquity, rebellion, and sin. But he will not leave the guilty unpunished, bringing the consequences of the fathers' iniquity on the children and grandchildren to the third and fourth generation.

MATTHEW 25:31–46

THE SHEEP AND THE GOATS

[31] "When the Son of Man comes in his glory, and all the angels with him, then he will sit on his glorious throne. [32] All the nations will be gathered before him, and he will separate them one from another, just as a shepherd separates the sheep from the goats. [33] He will put the sheep on his right and the goats on the left. [34] Then the King will say to those on his right, 'Come, you who are blessed by my Father; inherit the kingdom prepared for you from the foundation of the world.

[35] "'For I was hungry and you gave me something to eat; I was thirsty and you gave me something to drink; I was a stranger and you took me in; [36] I was naked and you clothed me; I was sick and you took care of me; I was in prison and you visited me.'

[37] "Then the righteous will answer him, 'Lord, when did we see you hungry and feed you, or thirsty and give you something to drink? [38] When did we see you a stranger and take you in, or without clothes and clothe you? [39] When did we see you sick, or in prison, and visit you?'

[40] "And the King will answer them, 'Truly I tell you, whatever you did for one of the least of these brothers and sisters of mine, you did for me.'

[41] "Then he will also say to those on the left, 'Depart from me, you who are cursed, into the eternal fire prepared for the devil and his angels! [42] For I was hungry and you gave me nothing to eat; I was thirsty and you gave me nothing to drink; [43] I was a stranger and you didn't take me in; I was naked and you didn't clothe me, sick and in prison and you didn't take care of me.'

[44] "Then they too will answer, 'Lord, when did we see you hungry, or thirsty, or a stranger, or without clothes, or sick, or in prison, and not help you?'

[45] "Then he will answer them, 'Truly I tell you, whatever you did not do for one of the least of these, you did not do for me.'

[46] "And they will go away into eternal punishment, but the righteous into eternal life."

God is justice, and God will always act justly—not by compulsion from the outside but because that's the way He is Himself.

A. W. Tozer
The Attributes of God

Day 12

"I will restore the fortunes
of my people Israel."
AMOS 9:14

The Hope of Future Restoration

AMOS 9

FIFTH VISION: THE LORD BESIDE THE ALTAR

¹ I saw the Lord standing beside the altar, and he said:

> Strike the capitals of the pillars
> so that the thresholds shake;
> knock them down on the heads of all the people.
> Then I will kill the rest of them with the sword.
> None of those who flee will get away;
> none of the fugitives will escape.
> ² If they dig down to Sheol,
> from there my hand will take them;
> if they climb up to heaven,
> from there I will bring them down.
> ³ If they hide
> on the top of Carmel,
> from there I will track them down
> and seize them;
> if they conceal themselves
> from my sight on the sea floor,
> from there I will command
> the sea serpent to bite them.
> ⁴ And if they are driven
> by their enemies into captivity,
> from there I will command

> the sword to kill them.
> I will keep my eye on them
> for harm and not for good.

> ⁵ The Lord, the GOD of Armies—
> he touches the earth;
> it melts, and all who dwell in it mourn;
> all of it rises like the Nile
> and subsides like the Nile of Egypt.
> ⁶ He builds his upper chambers
> in the heavens
> and lays the foundation of his vault
> on the earth.
> He summons the water of the sea
> and pours it out over the surface of the earth.
> The LORD is his name.

ANNOUNCEMENT OF JUDGMENT

> ⁷ Israelites, are you not like the Cushites to me?
> This is the LORD's declaration.
> Didn't I bring Israel from the land of Egypt,
> the Philistines from Caphtor,
> and the Arameans from Kir?

⁸ Look, the eyes of the Lord GOD
are on the sinful kingdom,
and I will obliterate it
from the face of the earth.
However, I will not totally destroy
the house of Jacob—
    this is the LORD's declaration—
⁹ for I am about to give the command,
and I will shake the house of Israel
among all the nations,
as one shakes a sieve,
but not a pebble will fall to the ground.
¹⁰ All the sinners among my people
who say, "Disaster will never overtake
or confront us,"
will die by the sword.

ANNOUNCEMENT OF RESTORATION

¹¹ In that day
I will restore the fallen shelter of David:
I will repair its gaps,
restore its ruins,
and rebuild it as in the days of old,
¹² so that they may possess
the remnant of Edom
and all the nations
that bear my name—
    this is the declaration of the LORD; he will do this.

¹³ Look, the days are coming—
    this is the LORD's declaration—
when the plowman will overtake the reaper
and the one who treads grapes,
the sower of seed.
The mountains will drip with sweet wine,
and all the hills will flow with it.
¹⁴ I will restore the fortunes of my people Israel.
They will rebuild and occupy ruined cities,
plant vineyards and drink their wine,
make gardens and eat their produce.
¹⁵ I will plant them on their land,
and they will never again be uprooted
from the land I have given them.
The LORD your God has spoken.

🔖 GOING DEEPER

2 SAMUEL 7:15–16

¹⁵ "But my faithful love will never leave him as it did when I removed it from Saul, whom I removed from before you. ¹⁶ Your house and kingdom will endure before me forever, and your throne will be established forever."

PSALM 103:6–10

⁶ The LORD executes acts of righteousness
and justice for all the oppressed.
⁷ He revealed his ways to Moses,
his deeds to the people of Israel.
⁸ The LORD is compassionate and gracious,
slow to anger and abounding in faithful love.

⁹ He will not always accuse us or be angry forever.

¹⁰ He has not dealt with us as our sins deserve
or repaid us according to our iniquities.

HEBREWS 1:1–12

THE NATURE OF THE SON

¹ Long ago God spoke to our ancestors by the prophets at different times and in different ways. ² In these last days, he has spoken to us by his Son. God has appointed him heir of all things and made the universe through him. ³ The Son is the radiance of God's glory and the exact expression of his nature, sustaining all things by his powerful word. After making purification for sins, he sat down at the right hand of the Majesty on high. ⁴ So he became superior to the angels, just as the name he inherited is more excellent than theirs.

THE SON SUPERIOR TO ANGELS

⁵ For to which of the angels did he ever say,

You are my Son;
today I have become your Father,

or again,

I will be his Father,
and he will be my Son?

[6] Again, when he brings his firstborn into the world, he says,

And let all God's angels worship him.

[7] And about the angels he says:

He makes his angels winds,
and his servants a fiery flame,

[8] but to the Son:

Your throne, God,
is forever and ever,
and the scepter of your kingdom
is a scepter of justice.
[9] You have loved righteousness
and hated lawlessness;
this is why God, your God,
has anointed you
with the oil of joy
beyond your companions.

[10] And:

In the beginning, Lord,
you established the earth,
and the heavens are the works of your hands;
[11] they will perish, but you remain.
They will all wear out like clothing;
[12] you will roll them up like a cloak,
and they will be changed like clothing.
But you are the same,
and your years will never end.

CLOSING REFLECTION

Flip back through the daily annotations you made in this Study Book to guide your reflection.

Justice

What are specific ways Israel and the other nations experienced and practiced injustice?

What repeated patterns are present in these examples?

What was God's response to injustice?

Response

What patterns of injustice and unrighteousness have I seen, experienced, and practiced in my own life?

Righteousness

What are specific ways Israel and the other nations experienced and practiced unrighteousness?

What repeated patterns are present in these examples?

How was God's righteousness, and His call for His people to live righteous lives, present throughout Amos?

Where do I need to repent?

How can I move forward, reflecting God through the active pursuit of justice and righteousness?

Grace Day

Take this day to catch up on
your reading, pray, and rest
in the presence of the Lord.

Mankind, he has told each of you
what is good and what it is the
LORD requires of you: to act justly,
to love faithfulness, and to walk
humbly with your God.

Micah 6:8

Weekly Truth

Scripture is God-breathed and true.
When we memorize it, we carry His Word with us wherever we go.

**For this reading plan, we have worked to memorize Amos 5:24.
Spend some time today reviewing the verse, asking God to
use you in bringing justice and righteousness to the world.**

"But let justice flow like water, and righteousness, like an unfailing stream."

Amos 5:24

See tips for memorizing Scripture on page 76.

BENEDICTION

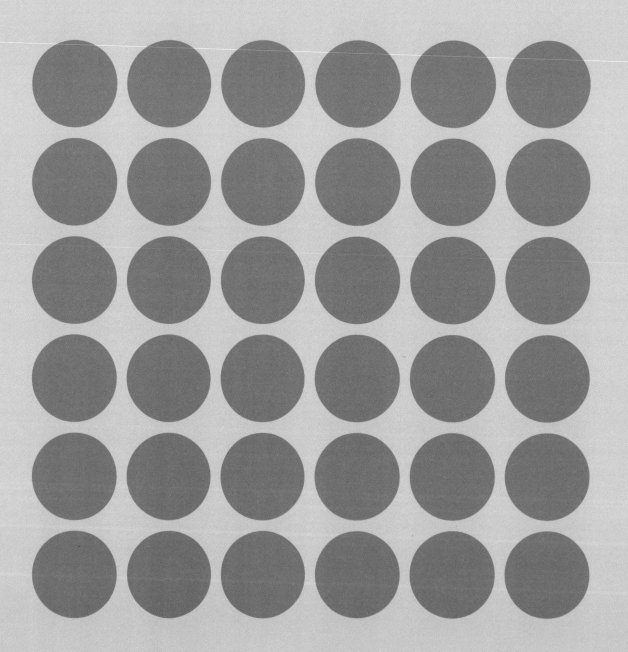

For the grace of God has appeared, bringing salvation for all people, instructing us to deny godlessness and worldly lusts and to live in a sensible, righteous, and godly way in the present age, while we wait for the blessed hope, the appearing of the glory of our great God and Savior, Jesus Christ. He gave himself for us to redeem us from all lawlessness and to cleanse for himself a people for his own possession, eager to do good works.

TITUS 2:11–14

Tips for Memorizing Scripture

At She Reads Truth, we believe Scripture memorization is an important discipline in your walk with God. Committing God's Truth to memory means He can minister to us—and we can minister to others—through His Word no matter where we are. As you approach the Weekly Truth passage in this book, try these memorization tips to see which techniques work best for you!

STUDY IT

Study the passage in its biblical context and ask yourself a few questions before you begin to memorize it: What does this passage say? What does it mean? How would I say this in my own words? What does it teach me about God? Understanding what the passage means helps you know why it is important to carry it with you wherever you go.

Break the passage into smaller sections, memorizing a phrase at a time.

PRAY IT

Use the passage you are memorizing as a prompt for prayer.

WRITE IT

Dedicate a notebook to Scripture memorization and write the passage over and over again.

Diagram the passage after you write it out. Place a square around the verbs, underline the nouns, and circle any adjectives or adverbs. Say the passage aloud several times, emphasizing the verbs as you repeat it. Then do the same thing again with the nouns, then the adjectives and adverbs.

Write out the first letter of each word in the passage somewhere you can reference it throughout the week as you work on your memorization.

Use a whiteboard to write out the passage. Erase a few words at a time as you continue to repeat it aloud. Keep erasing parts of the passage until you have it all committed to memory.

CREATE

If you can, make up a tune for the passage to sing as you go about your day, or try singing it to the tune of a favorite song.

Sketch the passage, visualizing what each phrase would look like in the form of a picture. Or, try using calligraphy or altering the style of your handwriting as you write it out.

Use hand signals or signs to come up with associations for each word or phrase and repeat the movements as you practice.

SAY IT

Repeat the passage out loud to yourself as you are going through the rhythm of your day—getting ready, pouring your coffee, waiting in traffic, or making dinner.

Listen to the passage read aloud to you.

Record a voice memo on your phone and listen to it throughout the day or play it on an audio Bible.

SHARE IT

Memorize the passage with a friend, family member, or mentor. Spontaneously challenge each other to recite the passage, or pick a time to review your passage and practice saying it from memory together.

Send the passage as an encouraging text to a friend, testing yourself as you type to see how much you have memorized so far.

KEEP AT IT!

Set reminders on your phone to prompt you to practice your passage.

Purchase a She Reads Truth 12 Card Set or keep a stack of note cards with Scripture you are memorizing by your bed. Practice reciting what you've memorized previously before you go to sleep, ending with the passages you are currently learning. If you wake up in the middle of the night, review them again instead of grabbing your phone. Read them out loud before you get out of bed in the morning.

CSB BOOK ABBREVIATIONS

OLD TESTAMENT

GN Genesis	**JB** Job	**HAB** Habakkuk	**PHP** Philippians
EX Exodus	**PS** Psalms	**ZPH** Zephaniah	**COL** Colossians
LV Leviticus	**PR** Proverbs	**HG** Haggai	**1TH** 1 Thessalonians
NM Numbers	**EC** Ecclesiastes	**ZCH** Zechariah	**2TH** 2 Thessalonians
DT Deuteronomy	**SG** Song of Solomon	**MAL** Malachi	**1TM** 1 Timothy
JOS Joshua	**IS** Isaiah		**2TM** 2 Timothy
JDG Judges	**JR** Jeremiah	**NEW TESTAMENT**	**TI** Titus
RU Ruth	**LM** Lamentations	**MT** Matthew	**PHM** Philemon
1SM 1 Samuel	**EZK** Ezekiel	**MK** Mark	**HEB** Hebrews
2SM 2 Samuel	**DN** Daniel	**LK** Luke	**JMS** James
1KG 1 Kings	**HS** Hosea	**JN** John	**1PT** 1 Peter
2KG 2 Kings	**JL** Joel	**AC** Acts	**2PT** 2 Peter
1CH 1 Chronicles	**AM** Amos	**RM** Romans	**1JN** 1 John
2CH 2 Chronicles	**OB** Obadiah	**1CO** 1 Corinthians	**2JN** 2 John
EZR Ezra	**JNH** Jonah	**2CO** 2 Corinthians	**3JN** 3 John
NEH Nehemiah	**MC** Micah	**GL** Galatians	**JD** Jude
EST Esther	**NAH** Nahum	**EPH** Ephesians	**RV** Revelation

BIBLIOGRAPHY

ESV Study Bible. Israel and Judah at the Time of Amos. Wheaton: Crossway, 2008.

Logos Bible Software. *Divided Kingdoms After Solomon and Other Kingdoms.* 2009.

LOOKING FOR DEVOTIONALS?

Download the **She Reads Truth app** to find devotionals that complement your daily Scripture reading. If you're stuck on a passage, hop into the community discussion to connect with other Shes who are reading God's Word right along with you.

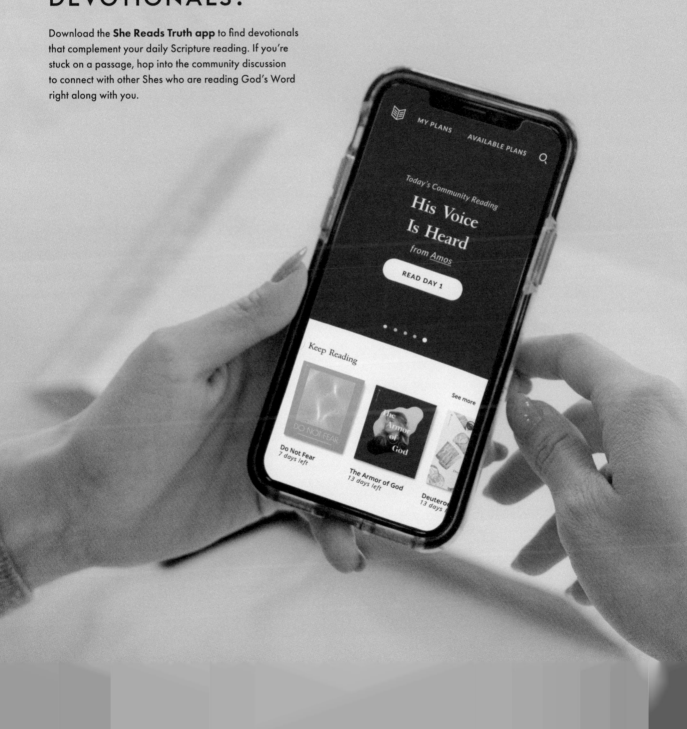

You just spent 14 days in the Word of God!

MY FAVORITE DAY OF
THIS READING PLAN:

HOW DID I FIND DELIGHT IN GOD'S WORD?

ONE THING I LEARNED
ABOUT GOD:

WHAT WAS GOD DOING IN
MY LIFE DURING THIS STUDY?

WHAT DID I LEARN THAT I WANT TO SHARE
WITH SOMEONE ELSE?

A SPECIFIC SCRIPTURE THAT
ENCOURAGED ME:

A SPECIFIC SCRIPTURE THAT
CHALLENGED AND CONVICTED ME: